The New Mum Hack Book

67 Tips and Tricks on Feeding, Changing, Sleep and Sanity

Published by Harding & Leslie
London N1 7GU
www.hardingleslie.com

DISCLAIMER

This book is not intended as a substitute for medical advice. It is for general information purposes only.

The statements made are not intended to diagnose, treat, cure, or prevent any condition or disease. The reader must consult with their own healthcare provider regarding the suggestions and recommendations made in this book.

Although the author and publisher have made every effort to ensure that the information in this book was correct at press time and, while this book is designed to provide accurate information in regard to the subject matter covered, the author and publisher assume no responsibility for errors, inaccuracies, omissions, or any other inconsistencies herein and hereby disclaim any liability to any party for any loss, damage, or disruption caused by errors or omissions, whether such errors or omissions result from negligence, accident, or any other cause. The author and publisher are not liable or responsible for any advice, course of treatment, diagnosis resulting from the use of this book.

This book provides content related to physical and/or mental health issues. As such, use of this book implies the reader's acceptance of this disclaimer.

For my Twinnie.
And my nephews A, E, & O.

CONTENTS

INTRODUCTION

Eat, sleep, poop. The Holy Trinity when it comes to parenting a new baby. Rumour has it that if you can get these three things right, your life will run oh-so-smoothly. As simple as it sounds, every parent of an infant will tell you, it's really not.

My kids were far from easy babies. Colic, reflux, eczema, constant breastfeeding, terrible sleep, food allergies, diaper rash...you name it, we had it. I seemed to have hit the motherlode and my sanity took a beating.

So, I got researching. I scoured parenting books and blogs, and interrogated dozens of parents, nurses and midwives as well. In this book, I've detailed the best tips, tricks and shortcuts I found. These were the ones that saved my life. They've helped countless other parents and I hope they will help you too.

There are more than 60 ideas, split into sections, for you to pick and choose when you need. There's information on optimising feeding and sleeping - for both baby and parents - as well as tips on everything from diaper rash to dealing with overwhelm.

This is by no means a comprehensive list. There are hundreds, perhaps even thousands, of hacks out there. The tips in this book are the ones that got the most votes from the mothers I interviewed. You will discover more through speaking to other parents, searching online and, of course, experimenting yourself.

Congratulations on your new baby. You can do this!

EAT

Feeding a new baby, particularly breastfeeding, can be very challenging. Issues with supply, latching and exhaustion are more common than you might think. This section has tips - proven time and again by many mums including myself - to make things easier.

In the meantime, remember that it can take months for you and Baby to work smoothly as a team. Hang in there. If needed, get help from a lactation nurse or the nearest chapter of La Leche League (www.llli.org).

1. No Booby Prize

We keep being told that "breast is best". Not only is this advice not true, it is dangerous. The phrase should be "fed is best".

If you are having trouble nursing in the first few weeks, don't give up. But equally don't be afraid to use some infant formula while you keep trying.

Remember that whether you choose to breastfeed or use formula, there is neither a Nobel Prize for Motherhood nor a shame-march through town. The most important thing is your child's health. Using infant formula could prevent your baby starving and getting dehydrated.

2. Eat, Drink and Be Milky

If you are choosing to breastfeed, you may find that making the right amount of breast milk is no easy feat. Doing everything you can to ramp up production in the early days after birth is key.

- Drink water, lots of it. Aim for a tall glass when you wake up and one every time you nurse your baby, as well as any time you are thirsty.

- Eat well. Your body needs fuel to make good milk and recover from childbirth. The body will prioritise recovery over milk production so you need enough reserves to do both. You can worry about losing the baby weight later!

Though obvious if you stop to think about it, this can be easy to forget in the early, hazy days after childbirth

Milk Machine

If the milk isn't coming in fast enough to keep baby sated (it rarely does), nature has a few catalysts. Fenugreek in particular is known to increase milk production in lactating mums. You must also make sure to drink enough water as mentioned previously.

3. 'Mother's Milk Tea' is a herbal tea containing fenugreek, blessed thistle, fennel and anise. It can be found in health food shops and online. The most effective method for using this tea requires an extra large mug and some dedication.

   - Steep one bag for 10 minutes in the morning, give it a squeeze, but don't throw out the bag. Drink up.
   - At lunchtime, add one more bag and steep the two bags, again for 10 minutes, before drinking.
   - In the evening, add a third bag to the two already in the mug and repeat. Then throw all the bags away when you're

done and start again the next day.

4. If herbal tea isn't your bag, you can use
    fenugreek capsules instead. These can be found
    in health food shops, online retailers and some
    supermarkets.

5. If the herbal route isn't working, discuss other
    options with your doctor. They may be able to
    refer you to a lactation nurse or have other
    recommendations including a prescription
    medication called domperidone. Not to be
    confused with the expensive champagne with a
    similar-sounding name, this medication
    stimulates the release of the hormone (prolactin)
    that drives milk production.

6. Tum towards Mum

If you are finding it difficult to get the baby to latch correctly (like every nursing mum I interviewed), check that she is not lying on her back with her head turned to the side, trying to feed over her shoulder.

Turn Baby's body towards yours and try again.

7. Sandwich

Imagine eating a sandwich. You hold it between your thumb and fingers and bring it up in line with your mouth to take a bite. Holding it perpendicular to your mouth (so that it runs along the length of your face) would be plain ridiculous right?

Sometimes latching issues are actually 'sandwich issues'. Make sure you're offering the breast in the right orientation. For example, if you're trying to latch while cradling your baby, hold the breast vertically from underneath, with the thumb on the inside and fingers on the armpit-side of your body, making a baby-mouth-sized sandwich to offer your hungry munchkin.

8. Hand Signals

A stressed baby, like some stressed adults, will have her hands clenched into fists. If you are wondering whether your little one has had enough milk, look at her hands. As she gets more and more full, her hands will get more relaxed.

9. Props to you

Whether you're feeding by breast or bottle you'll be doing it between eight and 30 (yes, thirty!) times each day. It can be physically and mentally demanding to say the least.

What might start as sore muscles and joints can, over time, develop into some pretty nasty injuries like pinched nerves in your neck or shoulders, carpal tunnel syndrome in your wrists or kyphosis in your spine that will give the Hunchback of Notre Dame a run for his money!

Could a well-placed cushion under your elbow or a pillow behind your back relieve some pressure? Or maybe you could prop one foot on a stool to provide some support. Would a neck pillow make all the difference? Experiment with a few props to see what works for you.

10. Body Scan

While you're at it, do a quick body scan as you are
holding Baby. Are you clenching your jaw or hiking up
your shoulders? Is your wrist and hand in a chicken
claw position? Just becoming aware should release
some of the tension and as a bonus you'll find you're
feeling less mentally tense too.

11. Reclined Goddess

Learning to nurse while lying on your side next to your baby can be a lifesaver as it allows you to get some much-needed rest. You may need to wait until your baby is around 4-8 months old to try this as your milk supply, as well as Baby's head control and ability to latch need to be firmly established.

12. Bra Liners

For a cheaper, thinner DIY alternative to conventional nursing pads, cut pantyliners to the right size and stick them to the inside of your bra.

This hack could also work to conceal 'smuggled peanuts' (protruding nipples) even if you are not breastfeeding.

13. DIY Pumping Bra

Using an electric breast pump to express milk can save your sanity. Doing this handsfree, without having to awkwardly hold the pump to your boob, while you have a meal or read a magazine can feel downright luxurious! You don't have to fork out on an overpriced specialist nursing bra for this. All you need is an old sports bra, a pen, pair of scissors and a mirror.

1. Put on your sports bra and look in the mirror.
2. Find where your nipples sit and mark here with an X.
3. Take off the bra and snip along the X.
4. Test with the breast shield (the cone-shaped piece of the pump that goes on the breast) making sure it just fits through the gap but is held snugly in place.
5. Adjust as necessary.

14. Freeze!

When freezing pumped milk in individual milk bags, ie the bags flat horizontally in the freezer. This has two dvantages.

1. You can stack them on top of each other so they take up less space in your freezer.
2. When the time comes to use them, the bags will defrost much faster.

15. Cover Girl

My kids hated being fully engulfed in a nursing cover. The few times I did try to use one while breastfeeding in public, they both pulled it off mid-feed leading to some serious flashing!

To save you the same embarrassment (and the hassle of buying and toting around something extra), tuck a scarf or muslin blanket under your bra strap on the side that you are feeding and let it drape across anything you want covered.

Nursing Tops No More

Nursing tops and dresses can be hard to find, costly and uncomfortable. Here are some ways to wear your regular tops, while preserving some modesty when you breastfeed in public. They work best with slightly loose tops.

16. Use maternity bands and maternity trousers to cover your stomach while breastfeeding, lifting up your top just enough for your little one to latch.

17. Camisole tops worn under a regular top are even better (and add some warmth in winter) as they leave nothing exposed. Lift up your top and pull down the cami just enough to create a little section for your baby to latch on.

Bonus: Matching the colour of the maternity band or camisole to either your top or bottom, makes it look so seamless that people may not even realise you are nursing!

18. Clip It

Through your breastfeeding journey, your boobs will grow enormously… and then they will shrink. While you wait to figure out what bra size you'll land on, you can use a large sturdy paper clip to make your bras tighter.

This is quicker and cheaper to find than bra strap clips, and stays in better. Just thread the paperclip through both the straps at the back, creating a racerback 'X', and adjust up or down as necessary.

19. Cluster Buster

There will be days when your baby will want to feed non-stop. This is called 'cluster feeding'. You'll see it in the early days as the baby tries to help you boost your milk supply by ramping up demand, as well as when he has a growth spurt. Lasting up to three days at a time, it can be exhausting both physically and mentally!

To survive:

- *Rest*: Take a nap whenever you can.

- *Let go*: Don't be a hero and try to keep up with any chores. Do the bare minimum and delegate where possible.

- *Fuel up*: Prioritise eating and drinking to keep your energy levels up.

- *Find entertainment*: Load your phone up with audiobooks, e-books, and magazines. Instead of giving in to the frustration that this period can bring, use it as a great time to binge-watch any shows that are on your list or read that novel you have been putting off.

20. Drive-Thru Milk

It can be heartbreaking when you're sitting next to your baby in the car and your little angel starts wailing in her infant car seat. You know some milk would soothe her but you are a long way away from your destination. Although you may feel desperate (and brave) enough to try to lean all the way forward and breastfeed - yes, one mum I interviewed did this! - it's neither safe nor ideal.

A tiny (30ml) bottle that you get with most breast pumps fitted with a slow-flow nipple could offer the relief you both need. Feed your baby very slowly, with a few drops at a time, giving her just enough milk to offer comfort but not so much that it is a choking risk.

21. Working Lunch

You may find you are on the job (feeding your baby) more often than not. Make sure you fuel up to keep your energy and mood lifted.

- Sandwiches and wraps are excellent on-the-go meals that are fast and easy to make, quick to eat and satisfying. Stock up on different fillings, condiments and sauces to get some variety in flavour and nutrition. You can even have sandwiches with one hand while you hold Baby in the other arm. Just make sure to wash your hands afterwards to prevent irritating Baby's delicate skin.

- Finger foods are a mum's best friend and so are things you can eat with just a fork or spoon. Stock up on cereal, microwaveable vegetables and food that is easily portionable like falafel, cheese, fish fingers, meatballs etc.

SLEEP

If there's something all parents of infants have in
common, it is the desperate desire for more sleep. The
tips in this section should help that dream become
more of a reality.

22. Setting Up for Good Sleep

The foundation to good sleep rests on three principles. The room should be

- Cool
- Dark
- Quiet

It is mind-blowing what a difference a fan, set of black out curtains and white noise machine can make to both Baby's sleep and yours. Tweak all three to get the right balance for you - think 'Goldilocks' and don't make it too cold to sleep, too dark to see or too quiet/loud.

Need tips on getting started? Read on.

Back-Up Black Out

If you're not keen on black out curtains, or want to test out the concept before you invest in some, here are some temporary options:

23. *Vinyl tablecloths*:

> These should be available easily and cheaply from your local dollar/pound store (or online). Use painter's tape, which doesn't leave a glue residue when removed, to secure them to your bedroom windows with the smooth plastic side facing into the room.

24. *Black garbage bags*:

> You likely have black bin liners at home already so could try this right away. Sturdy black bin liners work best as they are opaque and will not rip when repositioned or reused.
>
> Bear in mind that although this is a cheaper, more minimalist option than vinyl tablecloths, it

can be more time-consuming. Plastic garbage bags are slippery and you will need to line up several to cover each window.

To make this easier, tape a few garbage bags together on the floor to make the right shape and size as your windows, then secure them to your windows. Again painter's tape is your best option.

25. There's an App for That

Although a clip-on white noise machine can be a handy device for when you are out (just attach to the car seat or pram/stroller to drown out sound so you don't have to whisper) I prefer white noise apps. They are cheaper and much more versatile.

When our first child was an infant, my husband and I both got the paid version of White Noise Lite and put it on our phones, tablets and iPods. As apps are linked to Play Store and App Store accounts, years later we still always have white noise on us when the kids fall asleep.

'White' noise can sound a bit harsh and an app allows you to choose a different intensity (we use 'brown' noise), or a different background sound like rain or a vacuum cleaner.

26. Lazy Boy (or Girl)

There will be times when you are exhausted enough to keel over but Baby refuses to be put down. A reclining armchair will become your best friend.

Clip on a travel neck pillow around your neck and then prop the arm holding Baby onto a full-sized pillow so that if your arm goes limp, he will roll onto your chest and not the floor.

Never sleep with Baby in a sling or baby-carrier as it poses a suffocation risk.

27. Exhausted

Believe it or not, a (clean) bathroom can be an ideal place to get Baby to sleep. With the exhaust fan on and lights off, it can be cool and dark, with built in white-noise!

28. Latch-ing Issues

The last thing you want after finally getting Baby to sleep is for him to be woken by the click of the door latch.

Muffle this using a rubber band. Twist it into a figure 8, putting one loop over each door handle with the cross over the latch to push it in.

29. The Three S's to Sound Sleep

If you like Dr Harvey Karp's amazing method to get babies to sleep, here's my shortened and more intuitive version:

- *Snuggle*: Hold your baby snugly in your arms, with his arms tucked in (i.e. not flopping around) to prevent the startle reflex.

- *Shush*: Make a shushing sound in a rhythm you can sustain. I like taking one breath in then doing three short shush sounds - sshhh, sshhh, sshhh, <breath in>, sshh, sshhh, sshhh…

- *Sway*: Now sway side to side.

30. Roll Up, Roll Up

In order to help Baby feel like she is still being held once you've put her down, you can create a little sleep pod for her.

1. Get a king-sized duvet cover or layer two large bed sheets on top of each other.
2. Fold this lengthwise until you have a long strip that is roughly as wide as the length of your forearm.
3. Now, roll both ends of the long strip towards each other until you have approximately 12 inches between them.
4. Place this on the baby's bed with the smooth side up (rolls down). This will look like the voicemail symbol on your phone.
5. Flatten down the middle and place your sleeping angel in the little pod with her shoulders in line with the top of the rolls and her head out.
6. Adjust the rolls inwards or outwards until they are 'holding' her snugly.

31. New Mum Smell

If Baby has been extra clingy, putting a piece of your clothing next to him while he is sleeping may help. This must smell of Mummy so needs to have been worn against your body.

One idea is to slip off your t-shirt while putting Baby down and leave it near him (making sure it does not pose a suffocation risk of course!). Another idea, requiring fewer ninja skills, is to tuck a washcloth in your top for an hour or two before naptime and leaving that next to him in his crib when you put him down.

32. Perfect Timing

When you've finally managed to get your little one to sleep and are starting to fantasise about some shut-eye, the last thing you want to do is wake her as you put her down.

Luckily science has some guidance. Babies have shorter sleep cycles than adults and enter deep sleep roughly 20-30 minutes after they've fallen asleep. This is when they are least likely to be woken by a change in position, temperature etc. A new cycle begins with light sleep every 45 minutes or so.

Look at your clock when Baby has just nodded off and start counting down to freedom.

33. Balanced Transfer

If, instead of putting Baby down, you want to hand him over to another caregiver, make sure to keep him on the same side. This means transferring Baby from your left arm to Grandma's left arm, for example, so that Baby isn't woken by the abrupt change.

POOP

Babies poo. And pee. A lot. This means dealing with diapers will be a big part of your life for the next few years. Here are some helpful hints gathered from parents around the world.

34. Wet, Wet, Wet

Some diapers have a wetness-indicator line down the middle that changes from yellow to blue when Baby has done a pee. This can be a great help. Another way to tell is the 'pinch test' that's been tried and tested by generations of parents. A dry diaper will look more flat and feel crunchy when pinched. The more full the diaper, the more rounded its shape and more squidgy it is to the touch.

35. Chasing the Frill

When putting on a diaper make sure you run your finger along the leg holes to get the frills out. This will help prevent diaper leaks.

Simple? Yes. Effective? You bet!

36. Size Matters

Another key to preventing leaks (and clothes so soiled with poo that you're tempted to start a bonfire!), is to get the size of the diaper right.

The base of the diaper should cover the baby's entire bottom horizontally and the top of the diaper should reach the small of his (already small) back.

If we were to compare this to women's underwear, we would be aiming for control briefs and not bikini knickers. This may mean you need to size up before your child reaches the maximum weight printed on the pack of nappies.

37. Rash Decisions

Every baby gets diaper rash at least once. This happens because the acids from pee and poo break down their delicate skin. To prevent this, change diapers as often as necessary and make sure the diaper area is completely dry each time.

For added protection, apply a barrier like petroleum jelly, a diaper ointment containing zinc oxide or even coconut oil to the skin in the diaper area.

38. Wet Wipe

Baby poo is sticky stuff. The way to get it off the skin is not using more wipes or rubbing more vigorously but to use a more moist wipe.

When you know you'll be dealing with a stinky number two:

1. Arm yourself with one wet wipe that has been run under the tap for a few seconds, a pack of regular wet wipes (I like unscented, biodegradable ones) and some toilet paper or tissue.
2. As you open up the diaper, scrape off any excess poo-poo with a regular wipe (or the front half of the diaper).
3. Squeeze some of the water from your extra-wet wipe onto the diaper area and use the wipe to clean off any remaining excrement.
4. Do as many more rounds of wiping with regular wipes to get everything clean.
5. Blot the diaper area dry at the end with toilet paper or tissue and slather on diaper ointment.

39. Send Stains Down the Drain

If your baby is generating huge amounts of highly-stained laundry, then give yourself a pat on the back. She is eating and pooping well.

To save you from either using harsh chemicals or a lot of unnecessary elbow grease to get the stains out, keep a basin filled with a solution of water and gentle stain remover (I like both baking soda and the Babyganics range). Dump stained items into the basin as and when needed, and leave them to soak until the next time you do a load of Baby's washing.

Then pour out your solution and start again.

40. Baths

I have it on good authority (from a leading Canadian paediatric dermatologist) that you don't need to bathe your baby everyday.

Babies don't really sweat or get body odour. They don't touch door handles and light switches, or sit on bus seats. Unless it's been a particularly bad poo, or an all-out diaper blowout, a spot wash of anything that's icky or a full-body sponge bath will do.

Of course if your little one loves a bath as part of their bedtime routine, then go ahead and splash away.

41. A Breath of Fresh-ish Air

With all the cargo they carry, diaper bins can start to stink. Use a clip-on toilet freshener on the edge of yours to save retching every time you need to use it.

OUT & ABOUT

Leaving the house with your baby, whether to meet a friend or just run a tiny errand, can often seem like Mission Impossible. This section has a few tips to help you muster the courage to venture out.

42. Extra, Extra

Apart from having several diapers, any essential medication, and a snack for Baby and yourself, make sure you have spares of the following items:

- Wipes - one pack in your diaper bag and one in the caddy of your pushchair (stroller) that is easily accessible for quick clean ups
- At least one full outfit for baby in case of spit up, diaper leaks and other everyday disasters. This includes socks and mittens
- An extra t-shirt for you for the exact same reasons as above (hopefully Baby's mess and not yours)
- Bibs, washcloths etc

43. Band Aid

Roll up Baby's spare outfit and secure the bundle with a rubber band. Put this in a plastic bag, along with your spare bibs, washcloths and the extra t-shirt for you (also rolled and wrapped with a rubber band).

Any time you use these items, put the rubber band on your wrist to remind you to replace them for next time. Use the plastic bag to hold any soiled items.

44. Hanging Out

Clip a plastic over-the-door hook to your table to keep your diaper bag off dirty floors in restaurants and cafes. The hooks can be found easily and cheaply at most dollar/pound shops or online, and can work well to hold your non-baby handbag too.

45. Doggy Bag

For times when you are changing diapers on-the-go and there isn't a garbage bin nearby, keep a stash of dog-poop bags in your baby bag. These are the perfect size for one soiled diaper, as well as cheap and biodegradable too.

46. Clean Sweep

Diaper bags often end up housing everything and anything we might need. This means they can get pretty yucky inside.

For a quick and easy clean, use a sticky lint roller to remove crumbs, lint, and any other surprises that have been collecting at the bottom of your diaper bag.

SANITY & STYLE

Feeling overwhelmed? Join the club. Parenthood, particularly motherhood, can be a lot to handle. Don't worry friend, I've got your back. I've harnessed my skills as a yoga teacher and my world-leading expertise in being overwhelmed, and come up with the following tips to help you feel (and look) more like yourself again.

47. One, Three, Five

When you feel overcome with overwhelm, put your hands on your tummy and take one deep breath in and exhale fully, concentrating on how your hands are being moved up and down.

Next, name three things you can see, then three things you can feel, and three things you can hear.

Now, set the timer on your phone for five minutes and do any stretches or yoga postures that come to mind. No judgement. You don't have to look graceful, just keep going until the timer goes off.

48. The Mama Mantra

'This too shall pass'. If you haven't heard these four words already, you will.

Mums remind each other that although things can get insane, circumstances change pretty quickly. In the meantime, when things are spiralling out of control, repeat the mantra but put an emphasis on a different word each time:

This too shall pass
This **too** shall pass
This too **shall** pass
This too shall **pass**

Keep going until you are feeling better, trying different tones, pitches and accents if you like. Who knows, you might even make yourself laugh!

49. Uniform

Instead of pulling on any old mismatched loungewear you can find, consider adopting a uniform. Having just a few clothing items that all work together will aid your sanity (less decision fatigue) and your laundry burden. To keep the proportions balanced while you're working on your post-baby belly, try:

- Dark skinny jeans or leggings
- Loose top
- Slip-on shoes

Patterns on your top will hide stains, creases and 'smuggled peanuts' (protruding nipples). Plus, if everything is dark (or light, your choice!) you won't have to sort your laundry each time.

50. Super(wo)man

The schedule when looking after an infant can get gruelling. For times when you're feeling (and looking) like a zombie, faking it can help. No matter what you're wearing, you can feel somewhat pulled together with just three items:

- **Scarf**: Choose whether to tie this around your hair, wrap it as a chic turban, drape it around your neck or shoulders etc. You could even use one of Baby's muslin blankets instead if it's in a neutral colour and pattern!

- **Earrings**: Choose a pair big enough to make an impact on their own but not so big that Baby can pull on them easily.

- **Lipstick**: Nude or bold - your choice.

Keep these in your diaper bag and use one, two or all three as needed to quickly lift your look and your spirits whenever you need, either at home or out.

51. Brain Drain

As physically demanding as it can be to look after a young child, it can also be mind-numbingly boring (let's just call a spade, a spade).

If you're itching for more, this can be a good time to reignite social connections that have gone stale (using a messaging app, email or even real mail!). Meanwhile, puzzle apps like crosswords, sudoku etc can give your brain a bit of a workout.

If you're feeling extra adventurous, you could try a MOOC (massive open online course) app like EdX or Coursera. Or perhaps even write a book!

Set and Forget

With a new baby, a household, and countless other responsibilities, you have enough to juggle. Think of things you can automate. Here are some suggestions:

52. Set up subscriptions for things you buy regularly like diapers, wipes, sanitary pads and other toiletries, groceries etc. You'll save time and even some money.

53. Use a slow cooker and a rice cooker. Throw ingredients in them at the start of the day to have everything ready to go when you need.

54. A robot vacuum cleaner can work at night in the living areas, while you sleep, and clean the bedroom floors in the morning.

55. Nips and Lips

All that inevitable cluster feeding and shushing, can lead to cracked, sore nipples and dry lips. Lanolin-based nipple balm can be a life-saver here for both. Apply as often as needed for some much-needed healing.

Going Loco for Coco

Although I'm normally against any fads (and consider myself a *non-fluencer* on social media), I do love coconut oil. It's got as many uses as it has fans. Here are some reasons to have a tub of it in the house:

56. Skin

As a fruit oil (coconuts are not nuts!) it's a great all-over skin moisturiser for the entire family thanks to its medium-chain fatty acids. It's light and absorbs easily and has been shown to be good for eczema too.

57. Face

Although it is technically comedogenic (i.e. can block pores) I have used coconut oil as a one-step cleanser and moisturiser for years. When I want an extra cleansing boost, I add a few drops of tea tree oil to it before rubbing it on my face. I then wipe it all off with a cotton pad and splash my skin with cold water. Give it a try to see if it works for you.

58. Baby

Coconut oil works great for cradle cap (see Tip 66) and diaper rash (see Tip 37)

59. Food

Coconut oil can be used in baking as a healthy plant-based dairy-free alternative to butter. It's even delicious on toast!

60. Appy Days

Here is a list of smartphone apps that will make your life as a new parent run more smoothly:

- A white noise app (I use White Noise Lite)
- A feeding and diaper tracker (e.g. Feed Baby)
- A grocery shopping app for your region
- Amazon (Yes, I said it)
- Video streaming apps like YouTube, Netflix, Prime Video, Disney+ or whatever else floats your boat
- Reading apps like Kindle or Kobo for purchased books and Overdrive/BorrowBox/Hoopla for library books and magazines
- Messaging apps so you can vent to, I mean 'catch up with', friends and family
- A meditation app (go on, start a new habit that will change your life)
- A MOOC (massive open online course) app like Coursera or EdX for when you're ready to use your brain again

HEALTH

As much as we want our babies to always be rosy-cheeked, bouncing bundles of joy, there are times they will feel unwell. The key is not to panic and try unproven remedies found online. Contact your doctor or midwife with any concerns.

In the meantime, this section has tips on dealing with some very common ailments.

Reflux

All babies get some degree of reflux. This is because babies have tiny tummies and the sphincter (little rubber band-like structure) at the top of the stomach isn't strong enough at first to stop milk coming back up.

Reflux can be regurgitation (spitting up) after a feed or much more distressing for your baby. Here are some things you can do (using gravity's assistance) to help matters:

61. **Feeding**
   Feed Baby at a higher incline, i.e. less flat. Use props to help support you both as mentioned in Tip 9.

62. **Burping**
   Burp Baby more often during a feed to expel any air that she is swallowing along with milk. Don't go overboard however. Spend just a few minutes holding her upright against your torso while you pat her back gently. Do this halfway

through a feed, every time you switch sides and at the end of her meal.

63. Holding
Hold Baby upright for 30 minutes following each feed. This can be exhausting for you if you're feeding every two hours or so, but you may find it is worthwhile as it could allow your baby to avoid medication.

64. Changing
When changing Baby's diaper, instead of lifting up her legs so that she's doing a shoulder stand, roll her side-to-side while you slide the diaper underneath her.

65. Medication

There will be times when you need to give your baby
or toddler some medication. This may be anti-reflux
drugs, iron supplements, antibiotics or a number of
other things recommended by your doctor. Here's how
to do it:

1. Measure the correct dose into the syringe.
2. Cradle the baby in your lap if you can, with his
    head slightly elevated.
3. Put the tip of the syringe into the corner crease
    of his mouth, along the inside of the cheek, not
    in the centre. Putting the syringe in the centre of
    the lips will make the medicine hit the back of
    the throat and can cause choking.
4. Press the plunger of the syringe gently to
    administer 0.5-1ml of liquid.
5. Blow gently but quickly onto the child's face.
    This will induce the reflex to swallow.
6. Let the child catch his breath if needed and then
    repeat until you've given the full dose.

66. Cradle Cap

When your baby has thick, crusty, yellow scales
covering his scalp, it's hard not to be concerned. Both
my kids had cradle cap, with the second one being very
severe. I asked two paediatricians what to do. One
recommended aggressively combing the scales out
while the other suggested using Head & Shoulders
shampoo. I tried each strategy once and both seemed
painful for my child. There is a kinder way.

1. Warm a *small* amount of coconut oil until it is
   liquid (but not hot!).
2. Soak a cotton ball in it and gently dab onto the
   scales.
3. Once the oil has had a chance to soak in -
   perhaps at the next diaper change - wipe the
   scalp with a slightly damp washcloth, then dab
   the scalp with a dry washcloth to make sure
   Baby's head is dry.
4. If some scales come loose - lifted away from the
   scalp, NOT still attached - gently comb these
   out.

It may take weeks, or months, to resolve but I assure you that along with everything that is trying your patience at this time, this too shall pass.

67. Colic

Long bouts of unexplained crying in the evenings (colic) are more common for infants than you'd think.

In the past, it was thought that babies were distressed from a build up of gas during the day, and that diet was to blame. Research has shown that is very unlikely.

Colic is now thought to be related to the baby's nervous system adapting to the sudden increase in stimulation, including lights and sounds, after nine months in the quiet, dark womb.

Although distressing for everyone, colic tends only to last a few weeks while the nervous system matures. Here's what you can do in the meantime:

- Recognise your baby's colic schedule - what time does it usually start and how long does it usually last?

- Once you have noticed the pattern (isn't it amazing that there is an exact pattern?), take

Baby into a quiet, dark room with the white noise ten minutes before their colic start time and ride it out.

THE NEW MUM HACK KIT

- Mother's Milk tea or fenugreek capsules
- Cushions, step stool, neck pillow
- Pantiliners
- Old sports bra
- Scarves or muslin blankets
- Maternity bands and/or camisole tops
- Large paper clips
- Rubber bands
- Tiny baby bottle
- Black-out curtains or vinyl tablecloths/sturdy garbage bags
- Painter's tape
- Reclining armchair or nursing chair
- King-sized duvet cover or bedsheets
- Petroleum jelly or diaper barrier cream
- Coconut oil
- Nipple balm
- Baking soda or gentle stain remover

- Clip-on toilet freshener
- Plastic over-the-door hooks
- Dog poop bags
- Lint roller
- Medicine syringe
- Easy finger foods
- Uniform of choice
- Scarf, earrings and lipstick
- Slow cooker, rice cooker and robot vacuum cleaner
- Useful apps
- Patience

USEFUL RESOURCES

Breast Feeding:
Lactation consultants and support from La Leche League on https://www.llli.org

Sleep:
Articles and videos by Dr Harvey Karp on https://www.happiestbaby.com

Advice:
Science-based advice from a registered nurse and fellow mother at https://kellymom.com

ABOUT THE AUTHOR

Goldie Putrym loves solving puzzles. Ever since her first child was diagnosed with severe eczema and life-threatening food allergies, deciphering the complex conditions and helping others understand them has been her passion.

Goldie has an MEng in aeronautical engineering from Imperial College and an MA in journalism from City University London.

A true global citizen and polyglot, she has lived in Asia, Europe and North America. She currently resides in London, England, with her husband and two children.

ALSO BY GOLDIE PUTRYM

The Dairy Wheat Allergy Handbook

The Wheat Allergy Handbook

The Sesame Allergy Handbook

Printed in Great Britain
by Amazon

55679364R00056